SLOW DOWN
a minimalist coloring book

Special thanks to: God, Ashley, my family & friends, YOU

SLOW DOWN a minimalist coloring book by Todd Webb
www.toddbot.com

Published by Second House
www.second---house.com

Copyright 2016. All rights reserved.

ISBN 978-0-9861621-5-2

SLOW DOWN

Breathe

Look around you

Listen closely

be aware of your surroundings

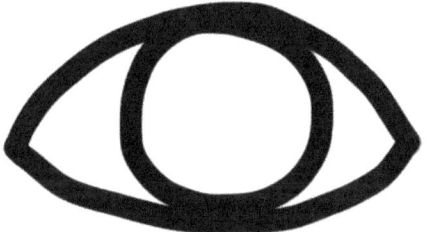

Focus

Waves or clouds?

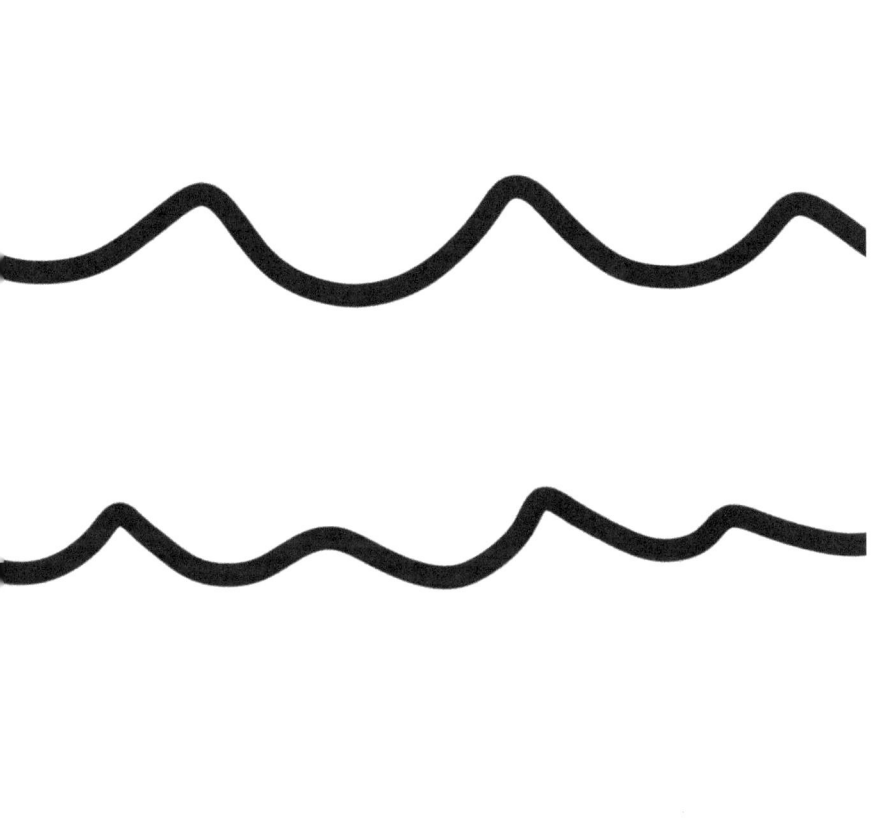

could this

this

be a

River?

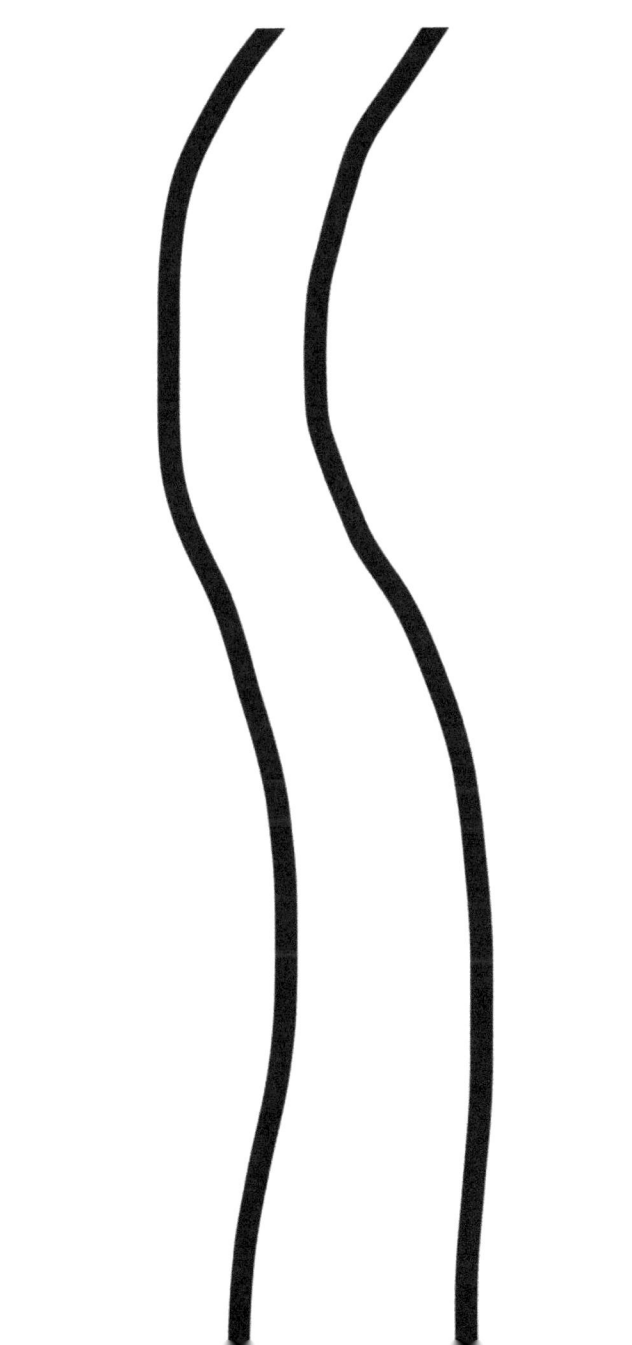

is this a waterfall?

OR the end of a rainbow?

seeds
oR
teaRs
oR
RaindRops?

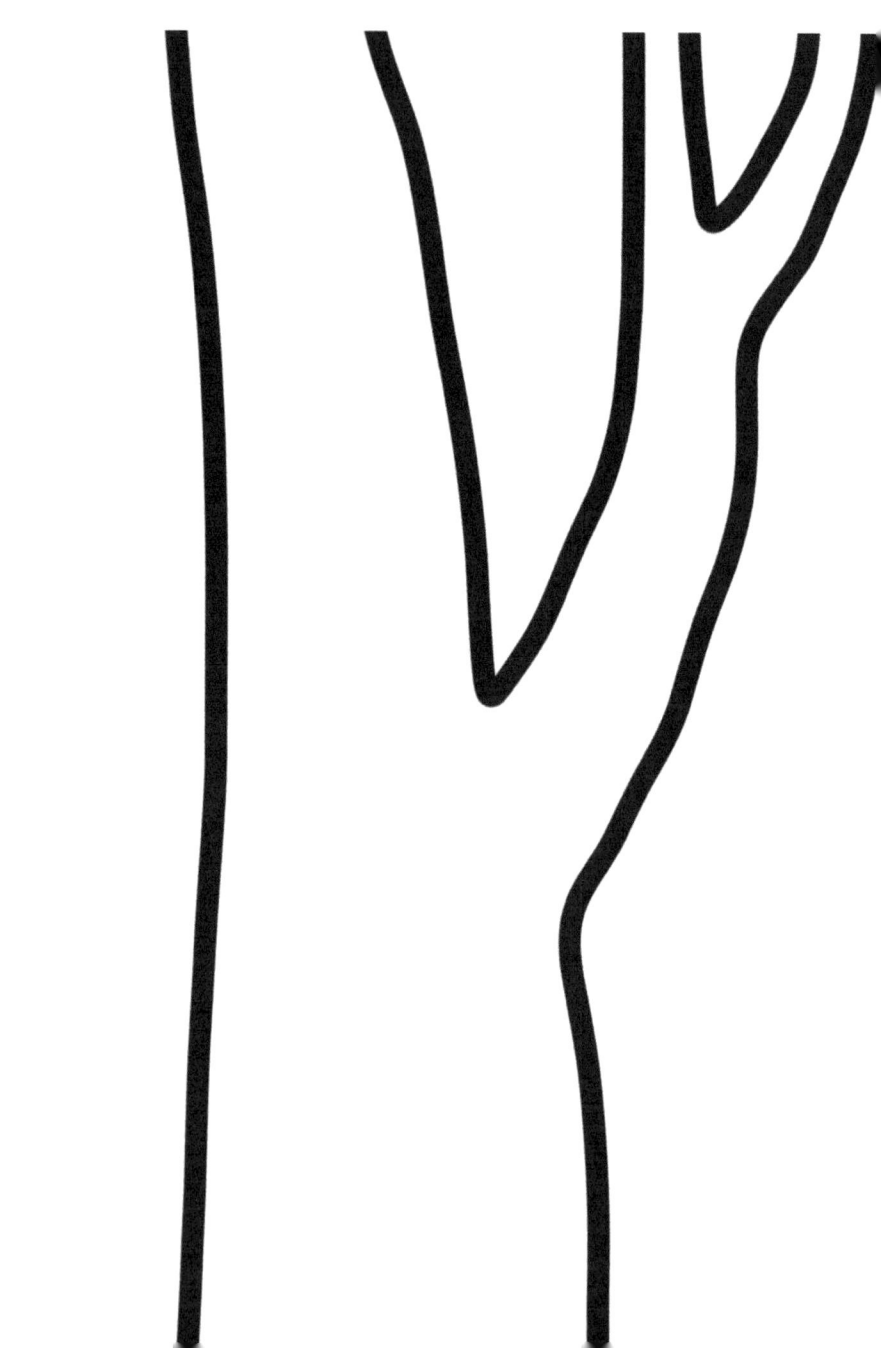

keep
it
simple

Take your time

COLOR
outside
the
Lines

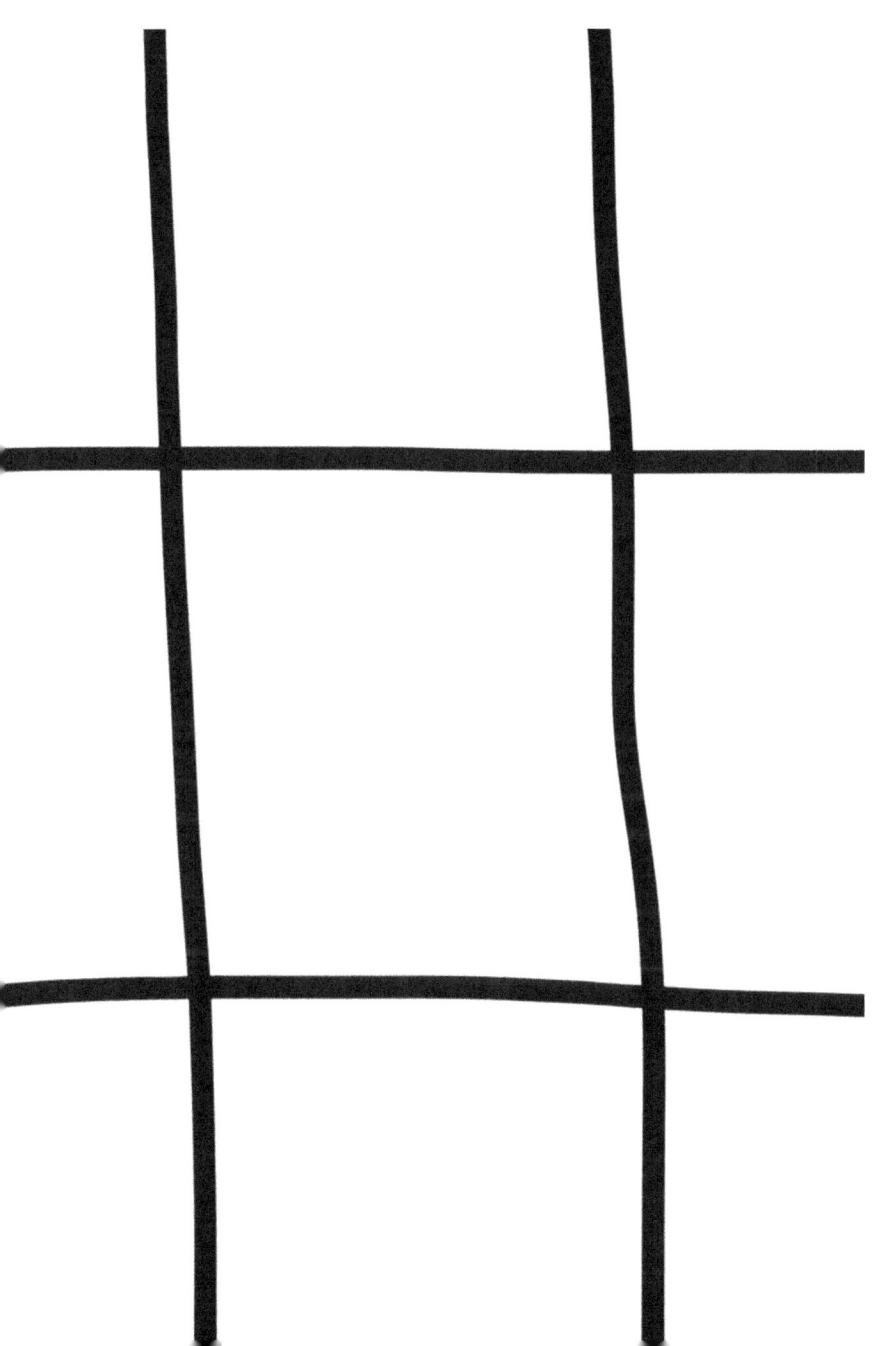

Could this be a swimming pool?

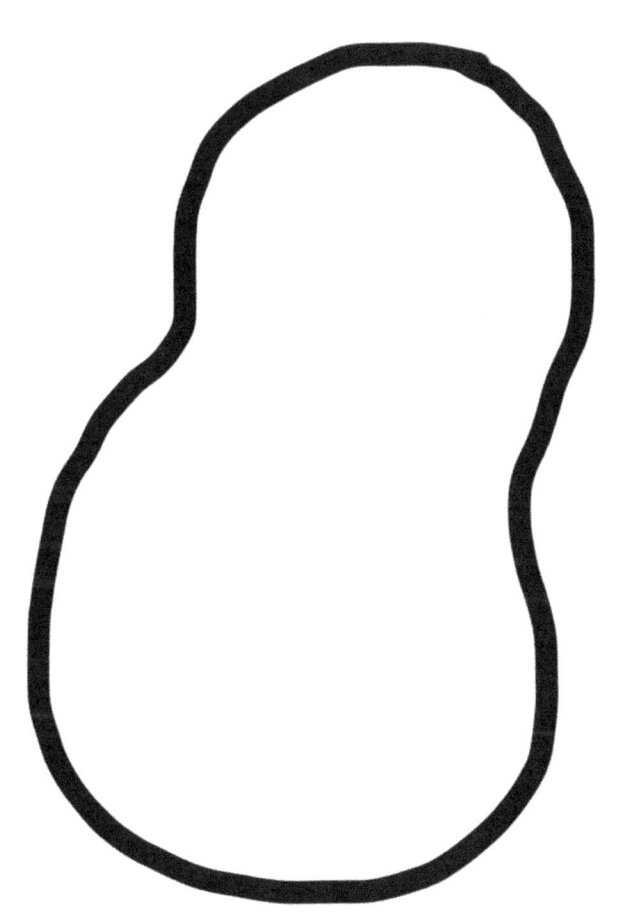

Is this a snowman or a peanut?

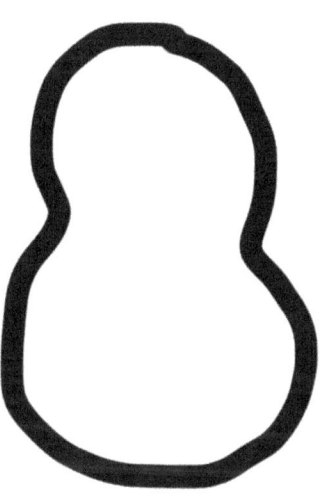

brown boxes or ice cubes?

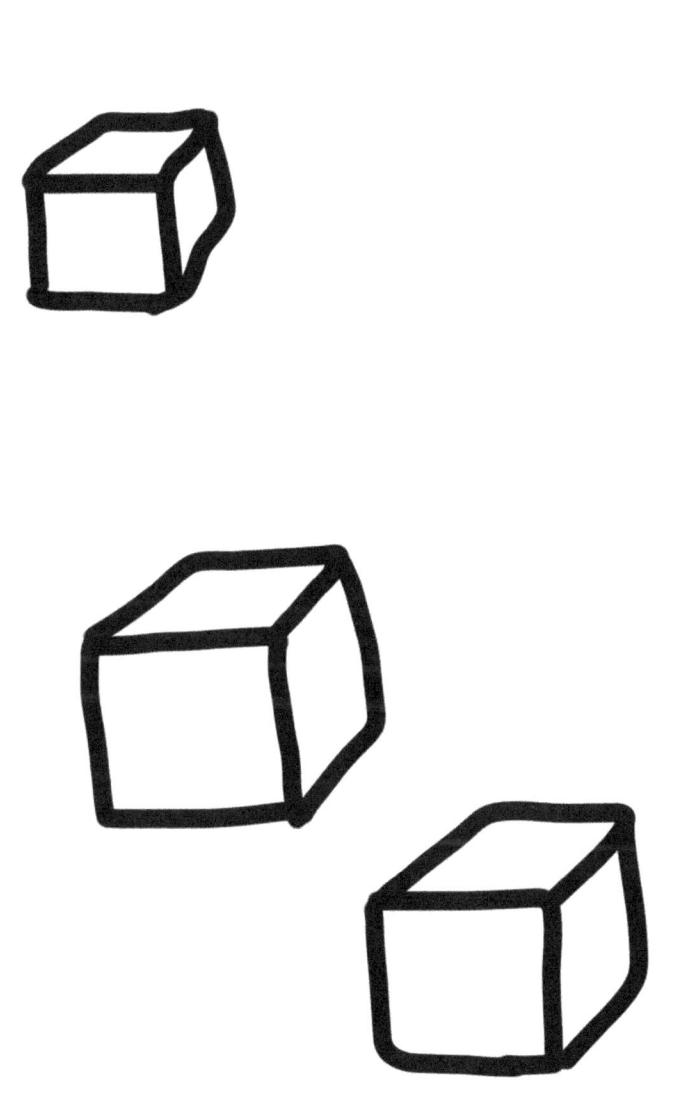

Be Still

COLOR
EVERYTHING
&
COLOR
NOTHING

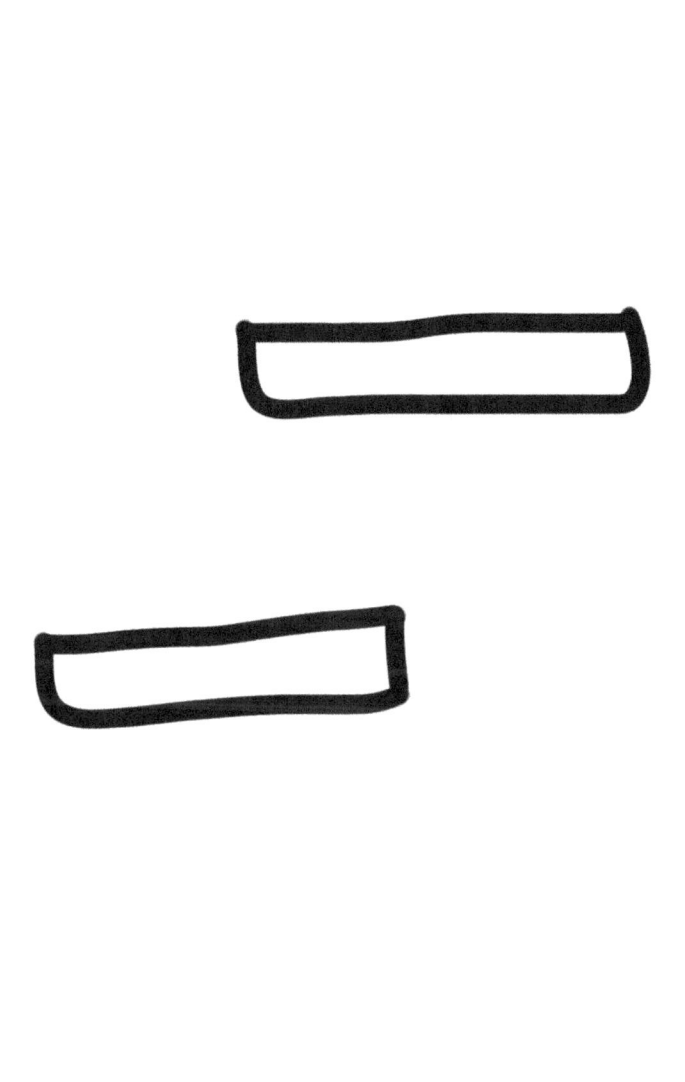

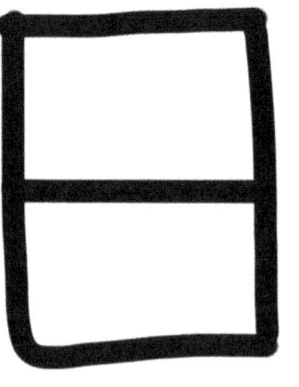

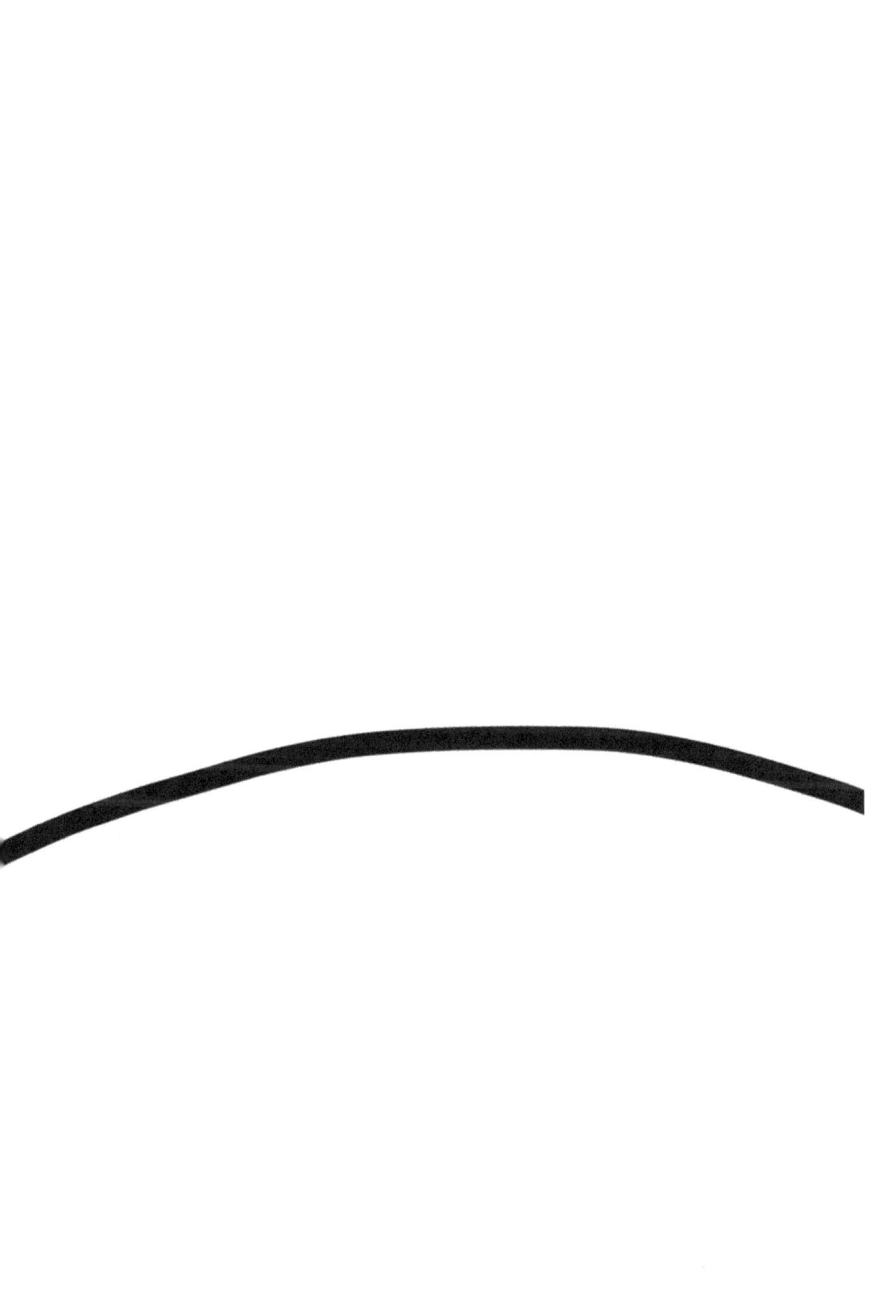

Palm trees or fireworks?

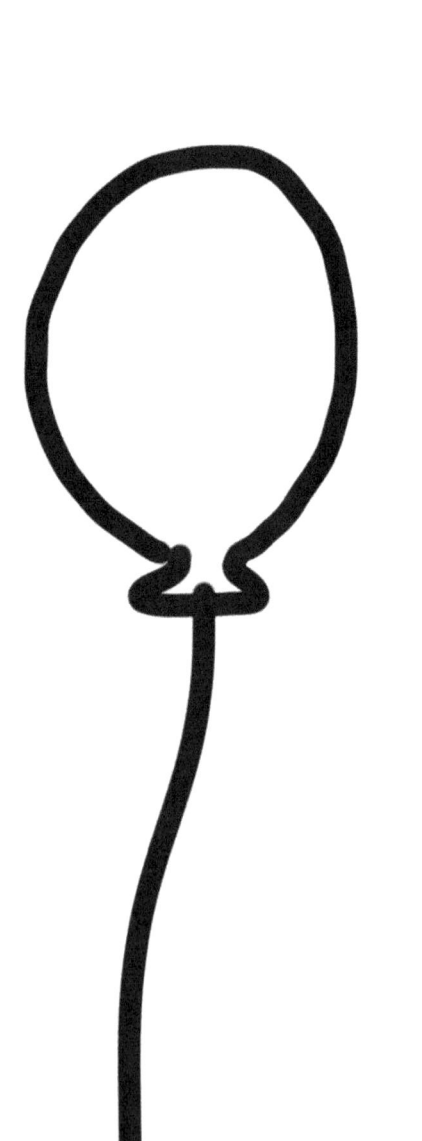

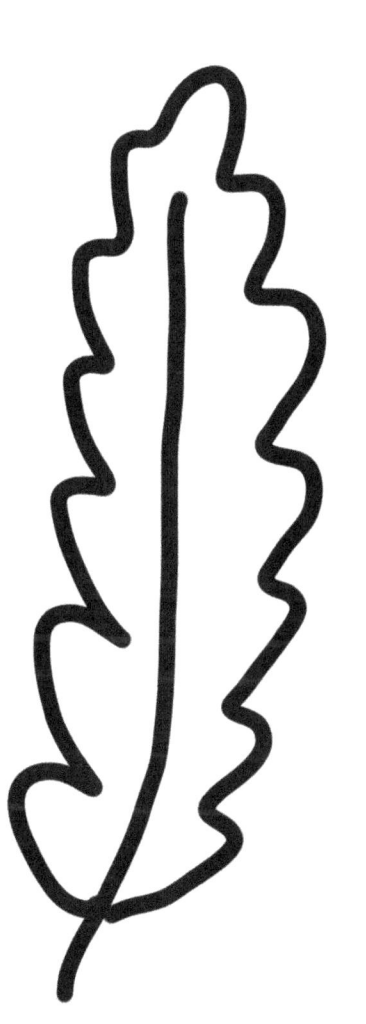

Change your way of seeing

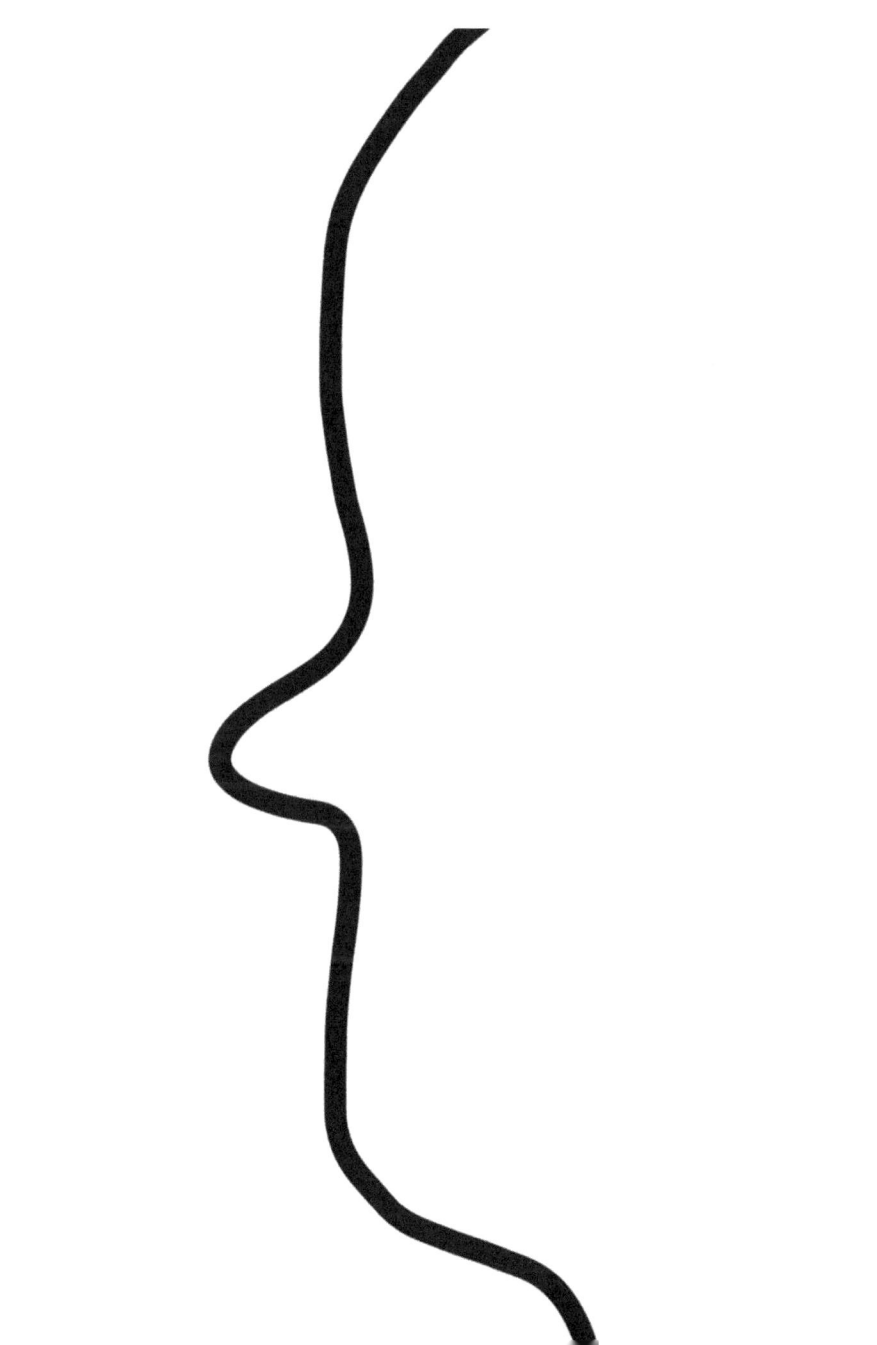

CLOUDS
OR
POPCORN
?

The Sun
or the
Moon?
Blue sky?
Sunset?

bubbles

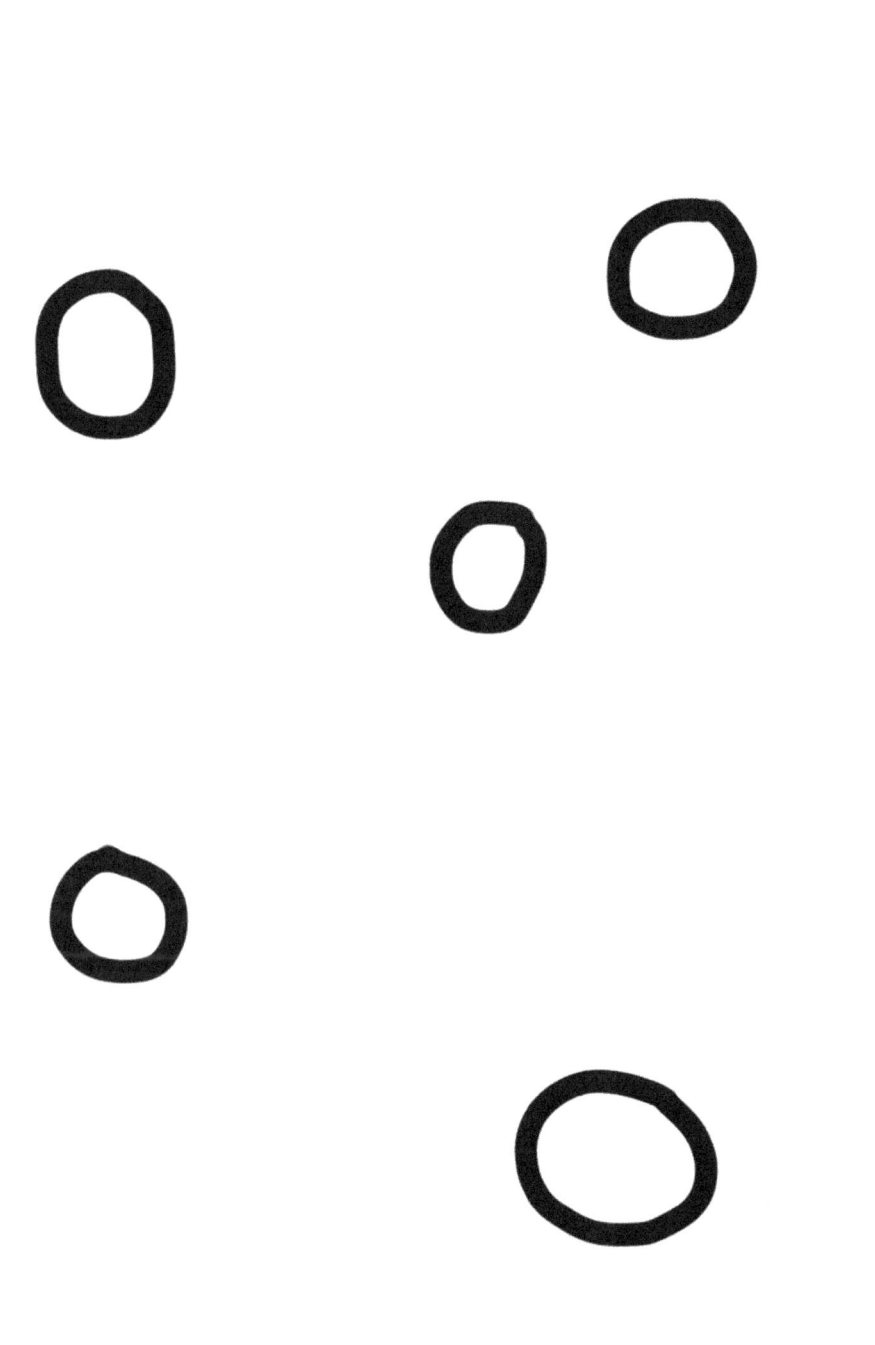

Snow flakes

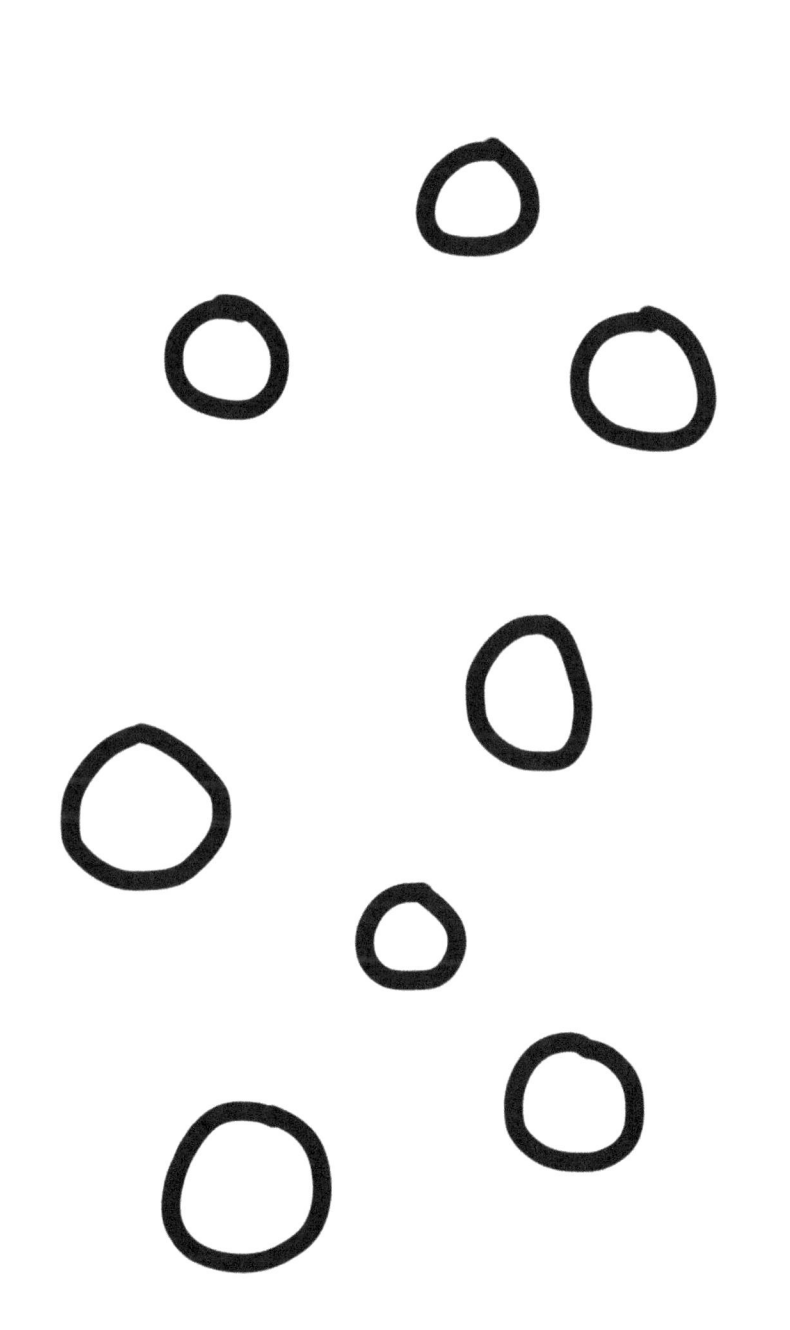

OR STARS?

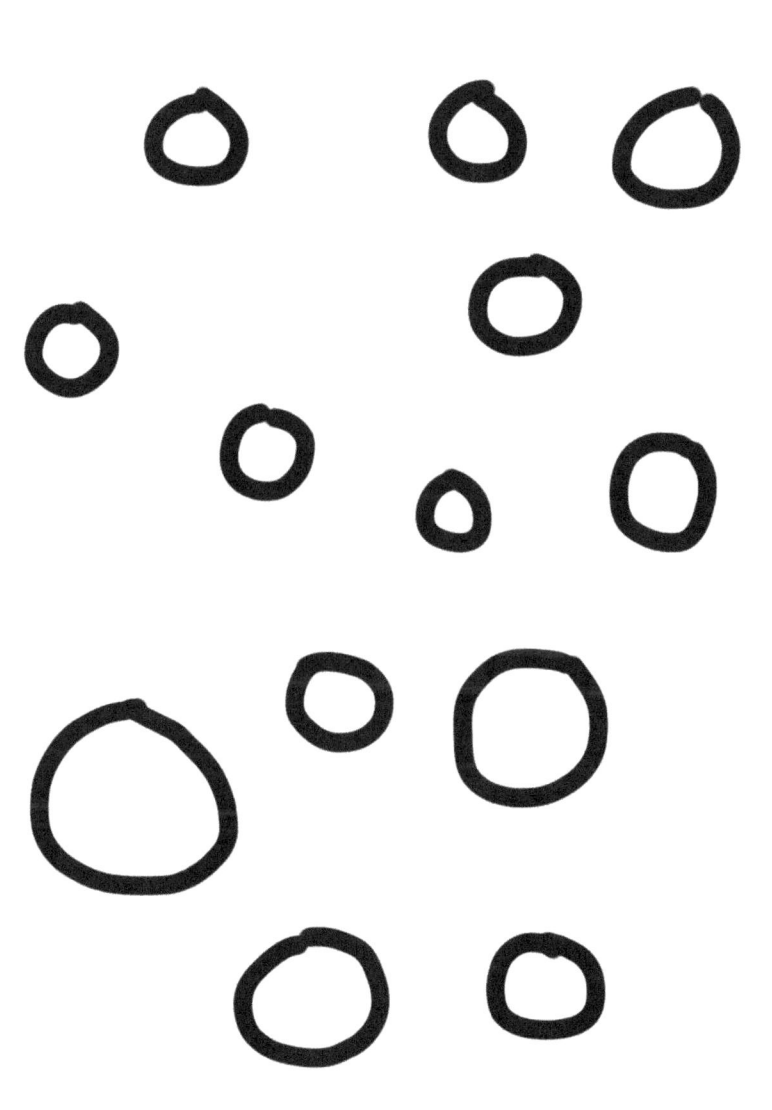

Is this the moon?

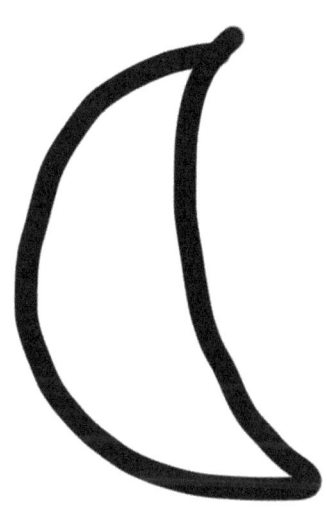

OR is it a banana?

Could it maybe be a toe nail?

Leaf
or
Feather?

Or is it
a whole
Tree?

grass growing or paint drying?

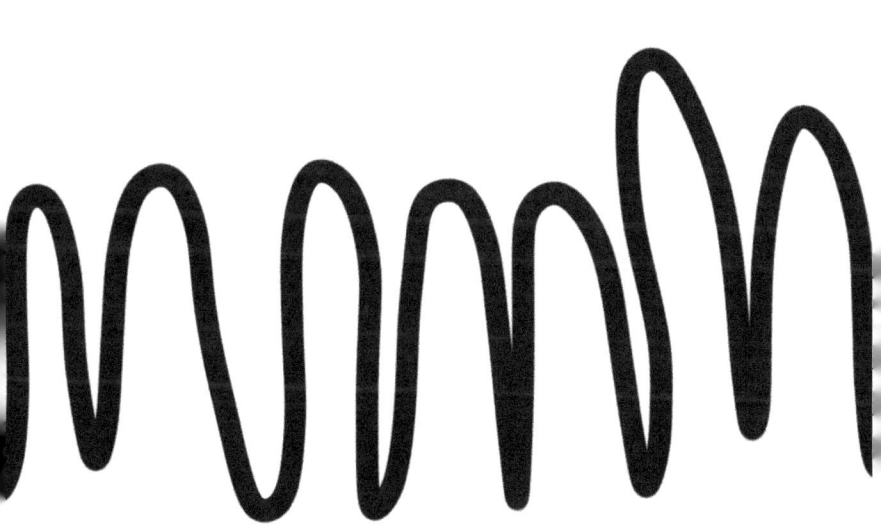

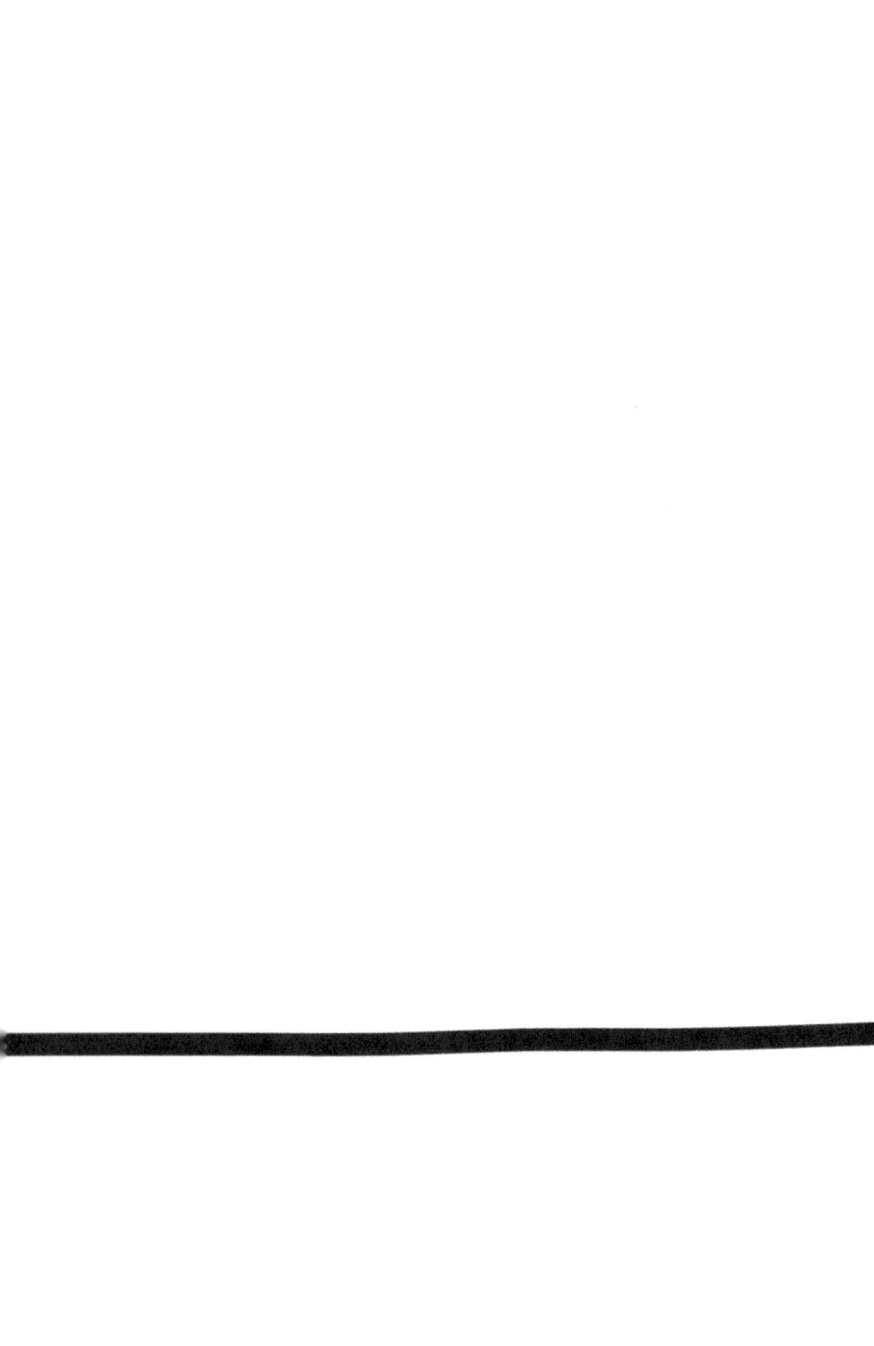

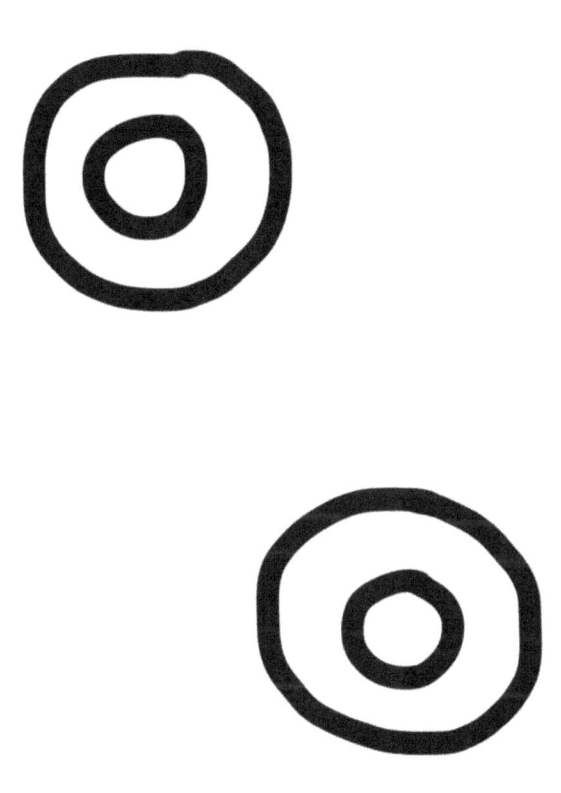

PURPLE
MOUNTAINS
?

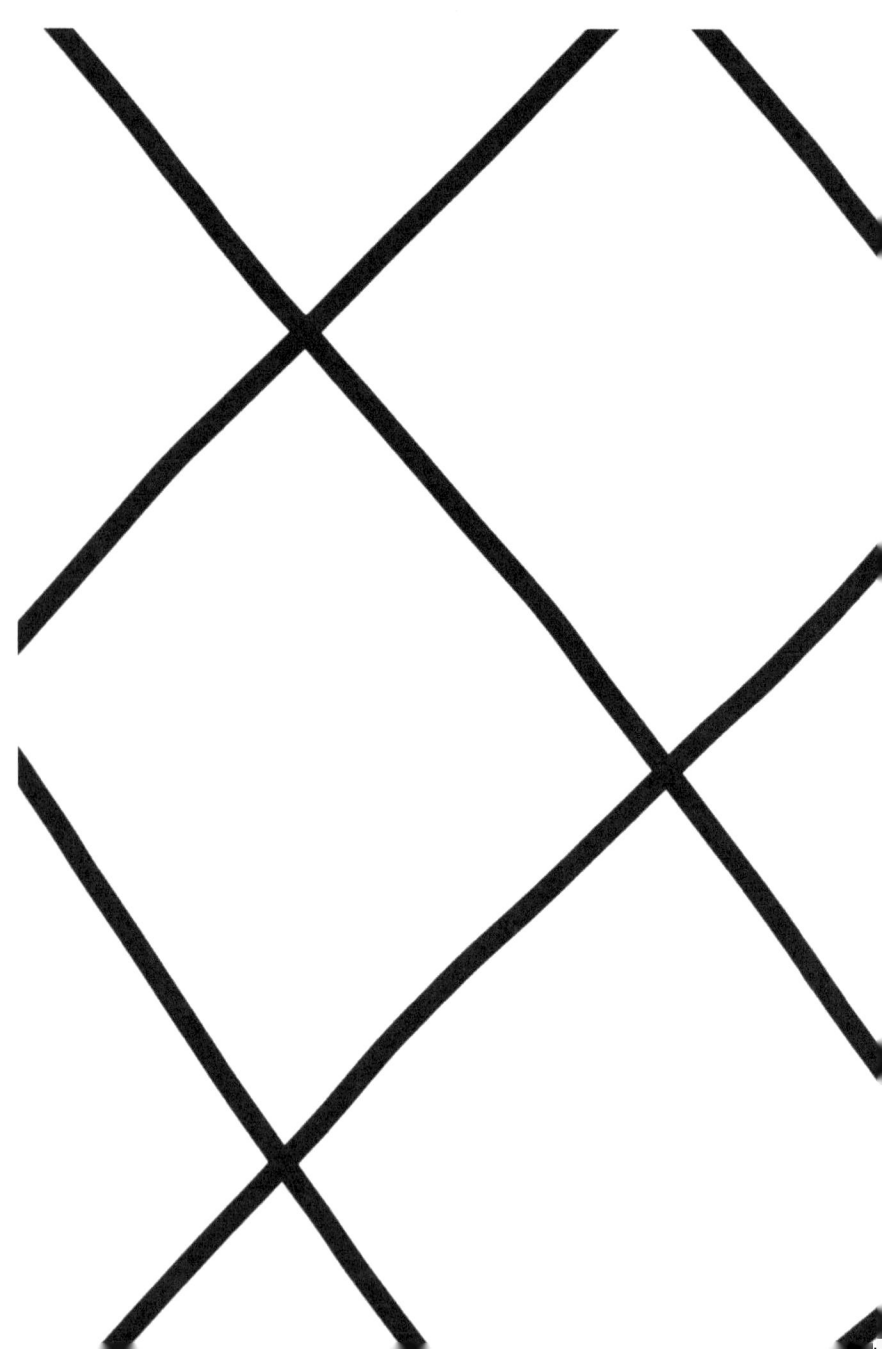

Be Content

Todd Webb was born in 1981.
He likes to make art about little moments and quiet things.
This is his first coloring book.

Other works include *The Goldfish & Bob*,
Tuesday Moon, *Casual Poet*,
Robbert Bobbert & the Bubble Machine,
Chance Operations, *The Woodlands*,
Valentine: A Cautionary Tale,
The Adventures of Danny & Mike,
and *Mr Toast Comics*. Webb performs music
under the monikers of Seamonster and
Oahu, and is always drawing.

To keep up with Todd or say hello, visit:
www.toddbot.com

www.ingramcontent.com/pod-product-compliance
Lightning Source LLC
Chambersburg PA
CBHW052029290426
44112CB00014B/2435